MW01172209

PRAYING SINNERS TO JESUS

How To Pray Effectively For The Lost

PAUL E CHAPMAN

Praying Sinners To Jesus

How To Pray Effectively For The Lost

By Paul E Chapman

Published by:
Add To Your Faith Publications
P.O. Box 5369
S. Kingstown, RI, USA

Bulk Discounts Available At AddToYourFaith.com.

Printed in USA

WELL DONE!

You are reading this book because you have a burden to see people saved. This book is an excerpt from a larger work entitled "Winning Souls God's Way: A Manual For Confident Soul Winning."

If you would like to further your soul-winning training to increase your effectiveness winning the lost, you can purchase the entire soul-winning manual at AddToYourFaith. com. It will be available in the Fall of 2023.

May Almighty God empower you to see many souls saved for His eternal glory!

LET'S CONNECT...

You can connect with the author by subscribing to updates at **PaulEChapman.com** and following him on social media platforms by the handle **@thepaulechapman**.

1

Praying For Sinners

Every genuine Christian has a desire to see lost sinners come to saving faith in Christ. We pray for their souls, pass out Gospel tracts, tell them about Jesus, and invite them to church. Yet, multitudes of sinners march on toward eternal destruction despite all our efforts.

Are we missing something? What if there was a simple, yet powerful, change we could employ that would make all the difference in our soul-winning efforts? This book is an answer to those questions.

Christ commissioned His disciples to preach the Gospel to every creature. Each generation of believers must seek to win the lost by preaching the saving power of faith in the death, burial, and resurrection of Jesus Christ. Glorifying God through the salvation of souls should be the highest priority of God's people.

1

Seeking the souls of lost sinners is the pinnacle of spiritual warfare. We cannot hope to be successful soul winners without prevailing prayer and supernatural power. This book will discuss the hopeless state of the lost, marvel at the miracle of salvation, and learn how to pray effectively for the lost to be saved.

Lost sinners will not be saved unless someone prays for them. How many lost souls have we failed to rescue because we have not labored in prayer for their souls? How many more needless deaths must occur before we grasp the holy urgency of praying for the lost to be saved?

God has given mankind an eternal soul and a free will. These gracious gifts separate us from the rest of creation. Every man, woman, and child has an eternal soul that will live forever in Heaven or die forever in Hell. Faith in the finished work of Christ is the only way to redeem a sinful soul and reserve its place in Heaven.

God has made salvation available to every sinner.

1 Timothy 2:4–6

Who will have all men to be saved, and to come unto the knowledge of the truth. For there is one God, and one mediator between God and men, the man Christ Jesus; Who gave himself a ransom for all, to be testified in due time.

God wants every sinner to be saved.

2 Peter 3:9

The Lord is not slack concerning his promise, as some men count slackness; but is longsuffering to us-ward, not willing that any should perish, but that all should come to repentance.

God leaves the choice of Heaven or Hell to each individual.

Revelation 22:17

And the Spirit and the bride say, Come. And let him that heareth say, Come. And let him that is athirst come. And whosoever will, let him take the water of life freely.

Sinners respond in one of two ways when they are confronted with the truth of Christ's Gospel.

1. Some will believe.

2. Some will not believe.

Acts 28:24

And some believed the things which were spoken, and some believed not.

Meditate upon this crucial question. Why would someone in their right mind reject God's free gift of salvation? The answer is simple... people in their right minds do not reject God's gift of eternal life! They receive it!

The Gospel makes sense. If there is a holy God Who must judge sin - and there is... If this holy God declares that unrepentant sinners must be separated from Him for eternity in fiery torment - and He does... If we know that we are imperfect sinners - and we do... If God sent His only begotten Son to die on the Cross to pay for our sins and rise again from the dead to conquer death - and He did... If this holy God offers to forgive our sin when we accept His only begotten Son as our Saviour - and He does... WHY WOULD ANYONE IN THEIR RIGHT MIND REFUSE SUCH A GIFT?

Accepting Jesus Christ as one's personal Saviour is the only logical choice when confronted with the facts!

Isaiah 1:18

Come now, and let us reason together, saith the LORD: Though your sins be as scarlet, they shall be as white as snow; Though they be red like crimson, they shall be as wool.

Here is the problem. Sinners do not think clearly. In fact, they are held captive by Satan. To make matters worse, the unredeemed are brainwashed by their spiritual captor, who makes sinners think they are free! With a form of "spiritual Stockholm Syndrome," sinners defend their condition, choosing to remain in bondage.

One of the great misconceptions of believers is that all we can do to win the lost to Christ is to share the Gospel. Of course, preaching the Gospel is necessary to fulfill The Great Commission! However, most believers do not understand their responsibility to pray for the lost nor the power of spiritual intercession for those in bondage to unbelief.

In this book, we will learn four vital truths about praying for the lost and discover specific prayer requests that supernaturally activate the power of prayer to see more people saved.

Let's get started!

2

Salvation Of The Lost Requires A Miracle

It is impossible to rescue a sinner from damnation without God's miraculous power.

The Bible explains that Satan blinds sinners. They cannot see the light of the glorious Gospel of Christ.

2 Corinthians 4:3–4

But if our gospel be hid, it is hid to them that are lost: 4 In whom the god of this world hath blinded the minds of them which believe not, lest the light of the glorious gospel of Christ, who is the image of God, should shine unto them.

You cannot logic a lost person to salvation. No well-designed argument, practiced persuasion, or carnal manipulation can regenerate the unrighteous.

You would have better luck describing the beauty of sunrise to someone born blind than explaining the miracle of salvation

5

to a lost man who is not under conviction.

Consider this testimony of salvation from the great preacher of the past, Charles Spurgeon.

"In my conversion, the very point lay in making the discovery that I had nothing to do but to look to Christ and I should be saved. I believe that I had been a very good, attentive hearer; my own impression about myself was that nobody ever listened much better than I did. For years, as a child, I tried to learn the way of salvation; and either I did not hear it set forth, which I think cannot quite have been the case, or else I was spiritually blind and deaf, and could not see it and could not hear it; but the good news that I was, as a sinner, to look away from myself to Christ, as much startled me, and came as fresh to me, as any news I ever heard in my life.

Had I never read my Bible? Yes, and I read it earnestly. Had I never been taught by Christian people? Yes, I had, by mother, and father, and others. Had I not heard the Gospel? Yes, I think I had; and yet, somehow, it was like a new revelation to me that I was to "believe and live." I confess to have been tutored in piety, put into my cradle by prayerful hands, and lulled to sleep by songs concerning Jesus; but after having heard the Gospel continually, with line upon line, precept upon precept, here much and there much, yet, when the Word of the Lord came to me with power, it was as new as if I had lived among the unvisited tribes of Central Africa, and had never heard the tidings of the cleansing fountain filed with blood, drawn from the Saviour's veins.

When, for the first time, I received the Gospel to my soul's salvation, I thought that I had never really heard it before, and I began to think that the preachers to whom I had listened had not truly preached it. But, on looking back, I am inclined to believe that I had heard the Gospel fully preached many hundreds of times before, and that this was the difference,–that I then heard it as though I heard it not; and when I did hear it, the message may not have been any more clear in itself than it had been at former times, but the power of the Holy Spirit was present to open my ear, and to guide the message to my heart....

Then I thought that I had never heard the truth preached before. Now, I am persuaded that the light shone often on my eyes, but I was blind; therefore I thought the light had never come there. The light was shining all the while, but there was no power to receive it. The eye-ball of the souls was not sensitive to the divine beams."

Consider God's Shocking Descriptions of the Wicked

The lost desperately need to be saved. It is impossible to understand how desperately lost sinners are without thoroughly studying the Scriptures. Even then, our imaginations are incapable of grasping their distance from perfection and the disgust of our Holy God toward sin.

In Scripture, the wicked are compared to:

1. Abominable Branches

Isaiah 14:19

But thou art cast out of thy grave like an abominable

7

branch, And as the raiment of those that are slain, thrust through with a sword, That go down to the stones of the pit; as a carcase trodden under feet.

2. Ashes Under the Feet

Malachi 4:3

And ye shall tread down the wicked; For they shall be ashes under the soles of your feet In the day that I shall do this, saith the LORD of hosts.

3. Bad Fishes

Matthew 13:48

Which, when it was full, they drew to shore, and sat down, and gathered the good into vessels, but cast the bad away.

4. Beasts

Psalm 49:12

Nevertheless man being in honour abideth not: He is like the beasts that perish.

2 Peter 2:12

But these, as natural brute beasts, made to be taken and destroyed, speak evil of the things that they understand not; and shall utterly perish in their own corruption;

5. Blind

Zephaniah 1:17

And I will bring distress upon men, that they shall walk like blind men, Because they have sinned against the LORD: And their blood shall be poured out as dust, and their flesh as the dung.

Matthew 15:14

Let them alone: they be blind leaders of the blind. And if the blind lead the blind, both shall fall into the ditch.

6. Briers and Thorns

Isaiah 55:13

Instead of the thorn shall come up the fir tree, And instead of the brier shall come up the myrtle tree: And it shall be to the LORD for a name, For an everlasting sign that shall not be cut off.

Ezekiel 2:6

And thou, son of man, be not afraid of them, neither be afraid of their words, though briers and thorns be with thee, and thou dost dwell among scorpions: be not afraid of their words, nor be dismayed at their looks, though they be a rebellious house.

7. Carcasses Trodden Under Feet

Isaiah 14:19

But thou art cast out of thy grave like an abominable branch, And as the raiment of those that are slain, thrust through with a sword, That go down to the stones of the pit; as a carcase trodden under feet.

8. Chaff

Job 21:18

They are as stubble before the wind, And as chaff that the storm carrieth away.

9. Clouds Without Water

Jude 12

These are spots in your feasts of charity when they feast with you, feeding themselves without fear: clouds they are without water, carried about of winds; trees whose fruit withereth, without fruit, twice dead, plucked up by the roots;

10. Corrupt Trees

Luke 6:46

And why call ye me, Lord, Lord, and do not the things which I say?

11. Deaf Adders

Psalm 58:4

Their poison is like the poison of a serpent: They are like the deaf adder that stoppeth her ear;

12. Dogs

Proverbs 26:11

As a dog returneth to his vomit, So a fool returneth to his folly.

Matthew 7:6

Give not that which is holy unto the dogs, neither cast ye your pearls before swine, lest they trample them under their feet, and turn again and rend you.

2 Peter 2:22

But it is happened unto them according to the true proverb, The dog is turned to his own vomit again; and the sow that was washed to her wallowing in the mire.

13. Dross

Psalm 119:119

Thou puttest away all the wicked of the earth like dross: Therefore I love thy testimonies.

14. Evil Figs

Jeremiah 24:8

And as the evil figs, which cannot be eaten, they are so evil; surely thus saith the LORD, So will I give Zedekiah the king of Judah, and his princes, and the residue of Jerusalem, that remain in this land, and them that dwell in the land of Egypt:

15. Fading Oaks

Isaiah 1:30

For ye shall be as an oak whose leaf fadeth, And as a garden that hath no water.

16. Fiery Oven

Psalm 21:9

Thou shalt make them as a fiery oven in the time of thine anger: The LORD shall swallow them up in his wrath, and the fire shall devour them.

17. Fools Building Upon the Sand

Matthew 7:26

And every one that heareth these sayings of mine, and doeth them not, shall be likened unto a foolish man, which built his house upon the sand:

18. Fuel For Fire

Isaiah 9:19

Through the wrath of the LORD of hosts is the land darkened, And the people shall be as the fuel of the fire: No man shall spare his brother.

19. Garden Without Water

Isaiah 1:30

For ye shall be as an oak whose leaf fadeth, And as a garden that hath no water.

20. Goats

Matthew 25:32

And before him shall be gathered all nations: and he shall separate them one from another, as a shepherd divideth his sheep from the goats:

21. Grass That will Be Cut Down

Psalm 37:2

For they shall soon be cut down like the grass, And wither as the green herb.

22. Idols That Can't Think

Psalm 115:8

They that make them are like unto them; So is every one that trusteth in them.

23. Melting Wax

Psalm 68:2

As smoke is driven away, so drive them away: As wax melteth before the fire, So let the wicked perish at the presence of God.

12

24. Moth-Eaten Garments

Isaiah 50:9

Behold, the Lord GOD will help me; Who is he that shall condemn me? Lo, they all shall wax old as a garment; the moth shall eat them up.

Isaiah 51:8

For the moth shall eat them up like a garment, And the worm shall eat them like wool: But my righteousness shall be for ever, And my salvation from generation to generation.

25. Passing Whirlwinds

Proverbs 10:25

As the whirlwind passeth, so is the wicked no more: But the righteous is an everlasting foundation.

26. Broken Pottery

Proverbs 26:23

Burning lips and a wicked heart Are like a potsherd covered with silver dross.

27. Raging Waves Of The Sea

Jude 13

Raging waves of the sea, foaming out their own shame; wandering stars, to whom is reserved the blackness of darkness for ever.

28. Reprobate Silver

Jeremiah 6:30

Reprobate silver shall men call them, because the LORD hath rejected them.

13

29. Scorpions

Ezekiel 2:6

And thou, son of man, be not afraid of them, neither be afraid of their words, though briers and thorns be with thee, and thou dost dwell among scorpions: be not afraid of their words, nor be dismayed at their looks, though they be a rebellious house.

30. Serpents

Psalm 58:4

Their poison is like the poison of a serpent: They are like the deaf adder that stoppeth her ear;

Matthew 23:33

Ye serpents, ye generation of vipers, how can ye escape the damnation of hell?

31. Smoke

Hosea 13:3

Therefore they shall be as the morning cloud, And as the early dew that passeth away, As the chaff that is driven with the whirlwind out of the floor, And as the smoke out of the chimney.

32. Stony Ground

Matthew 13:5

Some fell upon stony places, where they had not much earth: and forthwith they sprung up, because they had no deepness of earth:

33. Stubble

Job 21:18

They are as stubble before the wind, And as chaff that the storm carrieth away.

Malachi 4:1

For, behold, the day cometh, that shall burn as an oven; And all the proud, yea, and all that do wickedly, shall be stubble: And the day that cometh shall burn them up, saith the LORD of hosts, That it shall leave them neither root nor branch.

34. Swine

Matthew 7:6

Give not that which is holy unto the dogs, neither cast ye your pearls before swine, lest they trample them under their feet, and turn again and rend you.

2 Peter 2:22

But it is happened unto them according to the true proverb, The dog is turned to his own vomit again; and the sow that was washed to her wallowing in the mire.

35. Tares

Matthew 13:38

The field is the world; the good seed are the children of the kingdom; but the tares are the children of the wicked one;

36. Whited Sepulchres

Matthew 23:27

Woe unto you, scribes and Pharisees, hypocrites! for ye

are like unto whited sepulchres, which indeed appear
beautiful outward, but are within full of dead men's
bones, and of all uncleanness.

Wow! In each of these colorful descriptions we see the same themes repeated. Sinners are portrayed as corrupt, fruitless, vile, dirty, hopeless, and condemned. Only a miracle can save them from eternal damnation!

The bad news doesn't stop there. God continues to describe the wretched state of the lost in Scripture.

Consider The Hopeless Condition of the Lost.

1. Dead In Sins

   Ephesians 2:1

   And you hath he quickened, who were dead in trespasses and sins;

2. Aliens From God's People

   Ephesians 2:12

   That at that time ye were without Christ, <u>being aliens from the commonwealth of Israel</u>, and strangers from the covenants of promise, having no hope, and without God in the world:

3. Strangers From God's Promises

   Ephesians 2:12

   That at that time ye were without Christ, being aliens from the commonwealth of Israel, <u>and strangers from the covenants of promise</u>, having no hope, and without God in the world:

4. No Hope

Ephesians 2:12

That at that time ye were without Christ, being aliens from the commonwealth of Israel, and strangers from the covenants of promise, having <u>no hope</u>, and without God in the world:

5. Without God

Ephesians 2:12

That at that time ye were without Christ, being aliens from the commonwealth of Israel, and strangers from the covenants of promise, having no hope, <u>and without God</u> in the world:

6. Corrupt

1 Timothy 6:5

Perverse disputings of men of corrupt minds, and destitute of the truth, supposing that gain is godliness: from such withdraw thyself.

7. Blind

2 Corinthians 4:4

In whom the god of this world hath blinded the minds of them which believe not, lest the light of the glorious gospel of Christ, who is the image of God, should shine unto them.

8. Children of the Devil

John 8:44

Ye are of your father the devil, and the lusts of your father ye will do. He was a murderer from the beginning, and abode not in the truth, because there is no truth in him. When he speaketh a lie, he speaketh of his own: for he is a liar, and the father of it.

9. Under Authority of Satan

Acts 26:18

To open their eyes, and to turn them from darkness to light, and from the power of Satan unto God, that they may receive forgiveness of sins, and inheritance among them which are sanctified by faith that is in me.

10. Prisoners of War

Isaiah 14:17

That made the world as a wilderness, and destroyed the cities thereof; That opened not the house of his prisoners?

11. Bound by The Strong Man (Lucifer)

Mark 3:27

No man can enter into a strong man's house, and spoil his goods, except he will first bind the strong man; and then he will spoil his house.

12. Servants of Sin

John 8:34

Jesus answered them, Verily, verily, I say unto you, Whosoever committeth sin is the servant of sin.

13. Cannot Cease From Sin

2 Peter 2:14

Having eyes full of adultery, and that cannot cease from sin; beguiling unstable souls: an heart they have exercised with covetous practices; cursed children:

14. An Abomination To God

Deuteronomy 25:16

*For all that do such things, and all that do unrighteously,
are an abomination unto the LORD thy God.*

Scriptures make it clear that sinners are hopelessly lost
without Christ. Good intentions cannot change the nature
of a condemned soul. Good works cannot erase the stain of
sin. Religious actions cannot raise a dead spirit. The only
hope of salvation for lost sinners is the miracle of the new
birth!

John 3:1–7

*"There was a man of the Pharisees, named Nicodemus,
a ruler of the Jews: The same came to Jesus by night, and
said unto him, Rabbi, we know that thou art a teacher
come from God: for no man can do these miracles that
thou doest, except God be with him. Jesus answered
and said unto him, Verily, verily, I say unto thee, Except
a man be born again, he cannot see the kingdom of God.
Nicodemus saith unto him, How can a man be born
when he is old? can he enter the second time into his
mother's womb, and be born? Jesus answered, Verily,
verily, I say unto thee, Except a man be born of water
and of the Spirit, he cannot enter into the kingdom of
God. That which is born of the flesh is flesh; and that
which is born of the Spirit is spirit. Marvel not that I
said unto thee, Ye must be born again."*

3

Salvation Of The Lost Is The Pressing Desire Of Christ

God loves sinners despite their sin. Because of His great love for the lost world, God made a way of salvation.

John 3:16

For God so loved the world, that he gave his only begotten Son, that whosoever believeth in him should not perish, but have everlasting life.

Titus 3:4–7

But after that the kindness and love of God our Saviour toward man appeared, Not by works of righteousness which we have done, but according to his mercy he saved us, by the washing of regeneration, and renewing of the Holy Ghost; Which he shed on us abundantly through Jesus Christ our Saviour; That being justified by his grace, we should be made heirs according to the hope of eternal life.

1 John 4:8–10

He that loveth not knoweth not God; for God is love. In this was manifested the love of God toward us, because that God sent his only begotten Son into the world, that we might live through him. Herein is love, not that we loved God, but that he loved us, and sent his Son to be the propitiation for our sins.

Christ loves sinners. He proved His love for the lost by dying on the Cross for their sin.

Romans 5:8

But God commendeth his love toward us, in that, while we were yet sinners, Christ died for us.

Ephesians 5:2

And walk in love, as Christ also hath loved us, and hath given himself for us an offering and a sacrifice to God for a sweetsmelling savour.

1 John 3:16

Hereby perceive we the love of God, because he laid down his life for us: and we ought to lay down our lives for the brethren.

The Saviour did not simply love sinners from afar. Instead, He came to Earth to save them. The Jewel of Heaven was moved by His eternal love to leave the glories of Heaven to save His wayward creation. The Creator took on the form of His creation. The Limitless One took on the form finite man. The timeless God entered a world bound by time. The Sovereign relinquished His life to the whims of sinful men that He would judge one day. The Lord of life surrendered to death. Christ made all this sacrifice was made to save sinners.

Christ not only completed the sacrifice necessary for salvation, but also, He became the Gospel's greatest preacher. Christ spent three years walking through the Promised Land teaching the principles of His Kingdom, preaching the Gospel of salvation, and training men to spread His message to the ends of the earth.

Our Lord explained that He came to call sinners to repentance. Healthy people don't need a doctor, and perfect people don't need a Saviour. Sadly, the self-righteous Pharisees were blinded by pride, not seeing their need of Christ.

Matthew 9:13

But go ye and learn what that meaneth, I will have mercy, and not sacrifice: for I am not come to call the righteous, but sinners to repentance.

It is amazing that the Son of God would love sinners. It is astounding that He would come to earth to fulfill the Gospel plan and be the greatest preacher of the Gospel. Yet, there is even more reason to fall on our knees in worship. It is astonishing that Christ would seek sinners. Is it not enough that the Creator cares? Couldn't He have stopped with good reason at making salvation possible? Yet, our great Saviour actively seeks the lost!

I don't know how you came to Christ, but I do know one thing for sure. You didn't find Jesus. He found you! He sought you as a shepherd looking for a lost sheep. He sought you like a woman who searched for a valuable coin. He worked in your life in countless ways to bring you to Himself. He rejoiced when you were born again.

Luke 15:3–10

And he spake this parable unto them, saying, What man of you, having an hundred sheep, if he lose one of them, doth not leave the ninety and nine in the wilderness, and go after that which is lost, until he find it? And when he hath found it, he layeth it on his shoulders, rejoicing. And when he cometh home, he calleth together his friends and neighbours, saying unto them, Rejoice with me; for I have found my sheep which was lost. I say unto you, that likewise joy shall be in heaven over one sinner that repenteth, more than over ninety and nine just persons, which need no repentance. Either what woman having ten pieces of silver, if she lose one piece, doth not light a candle, and sweep the house, and seek diligently till she find it? And when she hath found it, she calleth her friends and her neighbours together, saying, Rejoice with me; for I have found the piece which I had lost. Likewise, I say unto you, there is joy in the presence of the angels of God over one sinner that repenteth.

Thank God for the seeking Saviour!

Christ's unquenchable love motivates Him to seek sinners.

Luke 19:10

For the Son of man is come to seek and to save that which was lost.

Some people believe that Christianity is not for them, thinking they belong to a group excluded from Christ's reach. Not so! Jesus Christ reached out to all people, seeking to save them.

Let's look at seven groups of people in the Bible that Jesus spent His time seeking.

1. Jesus Seeking The Jews

Matthew 15:22–24

And, behold, a woman of Canaan came out of the same coasts, and cried unto him, saying, Have mercy on me, O Lord, thou Son of David; my daughter is grievously vexed with a devil. But he answered her not a word. And his disciples came and besought him, saying, Send her away; for she crieth after us. But he answered and said, I am not sent but unto the lost sheep of the house of Israel.

This curious account of Scripture stands in contrast to the rest of the biography of Christ found in the Gospels. Most of the time, we see Christ Jesus tirelessly helping everyone He meets in His ministry. He even goes out of His way to help the sinful and suffering. Yet, in this story, our Lord ignores the pleas of a needy woman.

Finally, he explains why He refuses to help her. He was sent to the Jews first.

In the early church, the disciples only preached Christ to the Jews! God had to teach them that the Gospel was for everyone.

Acts 3:26

Unto you first God, having raised up his Son Jesus, sent him to bless you, in turning away every one of you from his iniquities.

In Acts chapter ten, God used a sincere gentile seeking God, Cornelius, to teach Peter that Gentiles could be saved.

Acts 10:34–35

25

Then Peter opened his mouth, and said, Of a truth I perceive that God is no respecter of persons: But in every nation he that feareth him, and worketh righteousness, is accepted with him.

Paul and Barnabas took the Gospel to the Gentiles after the Jews rejected it.

Acts 13:46

Then Paul and Barnabas waxed bold, and said, It was necessary that the word of God should first have been spoken to you: but seeing ye put it from you, and judge yourselves unworthy of everlasting life, lo, we turn to the Gentiles.

Some Jews believe in Jesus today. They are called Messianic Jews. God has not entirely cast away Israel.

Romans 11:1–5

I say then, Hath God cast away his people? God forbid. For I also am an Israelite, of the seed of Abraham, of the tribe of Benjamin. God hath not cast away his people which he foreknew. Wot ye not what the scripture saith of Elias? how he maketh intercession to God against Israel, saying, Lord, they have killed thy prophets, and digged down thine altars; and I am left alone, and they seek my life. But what saith the answer of God unto him? I have reserved to myself seven thousand men, who have not bowed the knee to the image of Baal. Even so then at this present time also there is a remnant according to the election of grace.

Romans 11:11–12

I say then, Have they stumbled that they should fall?

God forbid: but rather through their fall salvation is come unto the Gentiles, for to provoke them to jealousy. Now if the fall of them be the riches of the world, and the diminishing of them the riches of the Gentiles; how much more their fulness?

Romans 11:22–24

Behold therefore the goodness and severity of God: on them which fell, severity; but toward thee, goodness, if thou continue in his goodness: otherwise thou also shalt be cut off. And they also, if they abide not still in unbelief, shall be graffed in: for God is able to graff them in again. For if thou wert cut out of the olive tree which is wild by nature, and wert graffed contrary to nature into a good olive tree: how much more shall these, which be the natural branches, be graffed into their own olive tree?

God still loves the Jews. He is not done with them yet. He will work through them again during the tribulation period after the church is raptured.

Revelation 7:1–4

And after these things I saw four angels standing on the four corners of the earth, holding the four winds of the earth, that the wind should not blow on the earth, nor on the sea, nor on any tree. And I saw another angel ascending from the east, having the seal of the living God: and he cried with a loud voice to the four angels, to whom it was given to hurt the earth and the sea, Saying, Hurt not the earth, neither the sea, nor the trees, till we have sealed the servants of our God in their foreheads. And I heard the number of them which were sealed: and there were sealed an hundred and forty and four thousand of all the tribes of the children of Israel.

Even though most Jews reject Jesus Christ as the Messiah, we must seek to win them. Jesus came to them first. Jesus sought them first. The Gospel was preached to them first. We must seek them today.

2. Jesus Seeking The Gentiles

Christ had to come first to the Jews so prophecy could be fulfilled. However, His ultimate goal was to save Jews and Gentiles who would believe.

A gentile is anyone who is not a Jew. The Jews considered the gentiles pagans who could not be saved. They were seen as dogs and often treated that way.

Christ rebuffed the request of the gentile woman in our text. Yet, she did not give up easily! She compared herself to a dog who ate the crumbs from the Master's table and asked for help again.

Matthew 15:24–28

But he answered and said, I am not sent but unto the lost sheep of the house of Israel. Then came she and worshipped him, saying, Lord, help me. But he answered and said, It is not meet to take the children's bread, and to cast it to dogs. And she said, Truth, Lord: yet the dogs eat of the crumbs which fall from their masters' table. Then Jesus answered and said unto her, O woman, great is thy faith: be it unto thee even as thou wilt. And her daughter was made whole from that very hour.

The Saviour could not resist the humility and faith of this needy gentile woman. Our Lord's acceptance of her request and willingness to help her foreshadowed the fact that Christ's salvation is for everyone!

The Lord Jesus left Heaven to save sinners. He came to the Jews first. The Jewish nation rejected Christ as He knew they would. But He didn't just come for the Jews. He came to save everyone who would receive Him as the Saviour and believe the Gospel.

John 1:9–13

That was the true Light, which lighteth every man that cometh into the world. He was in the world, and the world was made by him, and the world knew him not. He came unto his own, and his own received him not. But as many as received him, to them gave he power to become the sons of God, even to them that believe on his name: Which were born, not of blood, nor of the will of the flesh, nor of the will of man, but of God.

We must seek the irreligious, pagan, and devotees to false religions. Jesus sought the gentiles. Christ died for everyone.

3. Jesus Seeking The Broken

Jesus did not come seeking the self-righteous who thought they had it all together. He is not looking for proud individuals seeking to proclaim their own righteousness.

Christ came for the broken, bruised, and bound.

Luke 4:16–21

And he came to Nazareth, where he had been brought up: and, as his custom was, he went into the synagogue on the sabbath day, and stood up for to read. And there was delivered unto him the book of the prophet Esaias. And when he had opened the book, he found the place where it was written, The Spirit of the Lord is upon me, because he hath anointed me to preach the gospel to the poor; he hath sent me to heal the brokenhearted, to preach deliverance to the captives, and recovering of sight to the blind, to set at liberty them that are bruised, To preach the acceptable year of the Lord. And he closed the book, and he gave it again to the minister, and sat down. And the eyes of all them that were in the synagogue were fastened on him. And he began to say unto them, This day is this scripture fulfilled in your ears.

Was anyone in the Bible more broken than the maniac of Gadara? This poor demon-possessed man lived in a cemetery, tormented by devils.

He was wild, dangerous, and separated from his community. He could not control himself nor be controlled by others.

Then Jesus came! After His encounter with Christ, He was a new man.

Mark 5:15

And they come to Jesus, and see him that was possessed with the devil, and had the legion, sitting, and clothed, and in his right mind: and they were afraid.

We must seek the broken and bruised. Christ can change their lives.

4. Jesus Seeking The Needy

God is full of compassion. He cares for the lost and needy.

Psalm 86:15

But thou, O Lord, art a God full of compassion, and gracious, Longsuffering, and plenteous in mercy and truth.

Christ had compassion for the sick and suffering. He expects us to seek and serve them even though they can do nothing for us in return. We serve God by seeking and serving the needy.

Matthew 25:32–39

And before him shall be gathered all nations: and he shall separate them one from another, as a shepherd divideth his sheep from the goats: And he shall set the sheep on his right hand, but the goats on the left. Then shall the King say unto them on his right hand, Come, ye blessed of my Father, inherit the kingdom prepared for you from the foundation of the world: For I was an hungred, and ye gave me meat: I was thirsty, and ye gave me drink: I was a stranger, and ye took me in: Naked, and ye clothed me: I was sick, and ye visited me: I was in prison, and ye came unto me. Then shall the righteous answer him, saying, Lord, when saw we thee an hungred, and fed thee? or thirsty, and gave thee drink? When saw we thee a stranger, and took thee in? or naked, and clothed thee? Or when saw we thee sick, or in prison, and came unto thee?

We must seek the needy as our Lord commanded us.

5. Jesus Seeking The Rich

The rich young ruler came to Jesus seeking eternal life. Read the sad story of his rejection.

Luke 18:18–25

And a certain ruler asked him, saying, Good Master, what shall I do to inherit eternal life? And Jesus said unto him, Why callest thou me good? none is good, save one, that is, God. Thou knowest the commandments, Do not commit adultery, Do not kill, Do not steal, Do not bear false witness, Honour thy father and thy mother. And he said, All these have I kept from my youth up. Now when Jesus heard these things, he said unto him, Yet lackest thou one thing: sell all that thou hast, and distribute unto the poor, and thou shalt have treasure in heaven: and come, follow me. And when he heard this, he was very sorrowful: for he was very rich. And when Jesus saw that he was very sorrowful, he said, How hardly shall they that have riches enter into the kingdom of God! For it is easier for a camel to go through a needle's eye, than for a rich man to enter into the kingdom of God.

Our Lord knew that this young man's riches were keeping him from God. The rich young ruler was relying on his riches far too much to trust the Saviour. Simple faith would have saved this wealthy man's soul, but he wasn't willing to stop trusting His wealth to save his life.

It is a sad fact that few rich people get saved. They trust their riches and see no need for the Saviour. Most wealthy Christians today were born again before they acquired riches.

It may be difficult for rich people to humble themselves to accept the Saviour, but it is not impossible.

Wealthy Zacchaeus was born again after meeting Christ.

Luke 19:2–10

And, behold, there was a man named Zacchaeus, which was the chief among the publicans, and he was rich. And he sought to see Jesus who he was; and could not for the press, because he was little of stature. And he ran before, and climbed up into a sycomore tree to see him: for he was to pass that way. And when Jesus came to the place, he looked up, and saw him, and said unto him, Zacchaeus, make haste, and come down; for to day I must abide at thy house. And he made haste, and came down, and received him joyfully. And when they saw it, they all murmured, saying, That he was gone to be guest with a man that is a sinner. And Zacchaeus stood, and said unto the Lord; Behold, Lord, the half of my goods I give to the poor; and if I have taken any thing from any man by false accusation, I restore him fourfold. And Jesus said unto him, This day is salvation come to this house, forsomuch as he also is a son of Abraham. For the Son of man is come to seek and to save that which was lost.

Joseph of Arimethea was a rich man who believed in Christ. God used him to request the lifeless body of Jesus, prepare Him for burial. Christ's body was placed in a tomb borrowed from Joseph.

Matthew 27:57–60

When the even was come, there came a rich man of

Arimathaea, named Joseph, who also himself was Jesus' disciple: He went to Pilate, and begged the body of Jesus. Then Pilate commanded the body to be delivered. And when Joseph had taken the body, he wrapped it in a clean linen cloth, And laid it in his own new tomb, which he had hewn out in the rock: and he rolled a great stone to the door of the sepulchre, and departed.

Jesus is still seeking and saving the wealthy. We must seek the rich in spite of their reliance on their wealth and position.

6. Jesus Seeking The Poor

Christ quoted a portion of Isaiah chapter sixty-one in His first public message.

The poor is listed first as those to whom the Saviour came to minister.

Luke 4:18

The Spirit of the Lord is upon me, because he hath anointed me to preach the gospel to the poor; he hath sent me to heal the brokenhearted, to preach deliverance to the captives, and recovering of sight to the blind, to set at liberty them that are bruised,

The Lord Jesus taught His disciples to take care of the poor and include them in ministry efforts. So many ministries overlook the poor because they cannot give anything back to the church.

Christ taught us to minister to the poor and God will give us rewards.

Luke 14:12–14

Then said he also to him that bade him, When thou makest a dinner or a supper, call not thy friends, nor thy brethren, neither thy kinsmen, nor thy rich neighbours; lest they also bid thee again, and a recompence be made thee. But when thou makest a feast, call the poor, the maimed, the lame, the blind: And thou shalt be blessed; for they cannot recompense thee: for thou shalt be recompensed at the resurrection of the just.

Never forget that the common people have always heard Jesus gladly! When you get discouraged, seek out a poor, broken, or common person to tell of Christ.

Mark 12:37

David therefore himself calleth him Lord; and whence is he then his son? And the common people heard him gladly.

We must seek the poor on the streets, in rescue missions, in subsidized housing, and depressed neighborhoods. A poor person still has an eternal soul for which Christ died.

7. Jesus Seeking Publicans & Sinners

The Jews hated publicans. They worked for the Roman government collecting taxes. Usually, they exacted more than was owed and kept the difference for themselves. Apostle Matthew was a tax collector whom Jesus sought and saved.

Mark 2:14–17

And as he passed by, he saw Levi the son of Alphaeus sitting at the receipt of custom, and said unto him, Follow me. And he arose and followed him. And it came to pass, that, as Jesus sat at meat in his house,

35

many publicans and sinners sat also together with Jesus and his disciples: for there were many, and they followed him. And when the scribes and Pharisees saw him eat with publicans and sinners, they said unto his disciples, How is it that he eateth and drinketh with publicans and sinners? When Jesus heard it, he saith unto them, They that are whole have no need of the physician, but they that are sick: I came not to call the righteous, but sinners to repentance.

Jesus was a friend of publicans and sinners. He did not spend recreational time with them partaking of their sin.

Instead, He built relationships with them to win their souls.

Sinners involved in open and gross sin often seem furthest from God. Yet, Christ commanded us to seek their souls.

Sinners know they are lost and need a Saviour. Often, conspicuous sinners are closer to salvation than the rich or self-righteous.

Matthew 21:28–32

But what think ye? A certain man had two sons; and he came to the first, and said, Son, go work to day in my vineyard. He answered and said, I will not: but afterward he repented, and went. And he came to the second, and said likewise. And he answered and said, I go, sir: and went not. Whether of them twain did the will of his father? They say unto him, The first. Jesus saith unto them, Verily I say unto you, That the publicans and the harlots go into the kingdom of God before you. For John came unto you in the way of righteousness, and ye believed him not: but the publicans and the harlots believed him: and ye, when ye had seen it, repented not afterward, that ye might believe him.

We must seek despised groups and open sinners. Christ died to redeem them from sin and deliver them from sinfulness.

There is no controversy. Jesus Christ came to seek and save sinners and delegated the job to us before He ascended to Heaven.

The Saviour did everything necessary to complete the Gospel plan and make salvation available to sinners. He passed the baton to His disciples before He ascended back to Heaven. Now, it is our responsibility to seek sinners. It is our burden to sacrifice our time, talent, and treasure in search of the lost.

Do you have the heartbeat of Jesus Christ? Do you care for multitudes who are one breath away from eternal damnation?

Do you love the lost more than the Devil hates them? Satan hates every human. He seeks to hurt God by taking as many people as possible who Christ loves to Hell with him. The Devil seeks to cheapen the sacrifice of the Saviour by hiding its worth from sinner. He is determined to rob Christ of the souls He purchased on Calvary by keeping lost souls from being saved.

We must fight against his evil designs through effective prayer for sinners and powerful preaching of the Gospel.

Prayer has been described as "love on its knees." A parent's love motivates them to pray without ceasing for their children. Christ is on the right hand of the Father interceding for His people. How much does our love for Christ or compassion for the condemned motivate us to pray for the salvation of lost sinners?

We will never reach our potential in winning lost souls until we learn to pray effectively for them to be saved.

4

Salvation Of The Lost Is Spiritual Warfare

Seeking and saving sinners is supernatural work. Once you obey Christ's command to pursue lost souls, you step onto a spiritual battlefield. The battle is over the souls of men. Satan wants to keep sinners blind and bound until they open their eyes in eternal fire. Christ wants to liberate them from bondage, giving them life eternal. We are the soldiers of Christ in this holy war.

Ephesians 2:2

Wherein in time past ye walked according to the course of this world, according to the prince of the power of the air, the spirit that now worketh in the children of disobedience:

Sinners walk in lockstep with the sinful world under the direction of the Devil.

1 John 5:19

*And we know that we are of God, and the whole world
lieth in wickedness.*

The whole world lies prostrate under the influence of Satan.
In his book, The Epistles of John, John R.W. Stott made the
following observation about this verse.

> *"It [the world] is 'in the evil one,' in his grip and
> under his dominion. Moreover, it lies there. It is not
> represented as struggling actively to be free but as
> quietly lying, perhaps even unconsciously asleep, in
> the arms of Satan. The evil one does not 'touch' the
> Christian, but the world is helplessly in his grasp."*

When Adam sinned in the Garden of Eden, his dominion
over the Earth passed to Satan. The Evil One is the "god of
this world" until Christ redeems creation by making a new
Heaven and a new Earth.

2 Corinthians 4:4

*In whom the god of this world hath blinded the minds
of them which believe not, lest the light of the glorious
gospel of Christ, who is the image of God, should shine
unto them.*

Additionally, Christ likened a sinner that needed help to the
possession of the strong man. Our Lord explained that the
sinner could only be freed if you first bind his captor.

Mark 3:27

*No man can enter into a strong man's house, and spoil
his goods, except he will first bind the strong man; and
then he will spoil his house.*

Satan uses two main tools to enslave the lost.

1. Sins of the Flesh.

Sin provides just enough pleasure to distract a sinner from its consequences and entrap the unrighteous in a vicious cycle of pleasure and pain.

Meditate upon this shocking verse.

Revelation 21:8

But the fearful, and unbelieving, and the abominable, and murderers, and whoremongers, and sorcerers, and idolaters, and all liars, shall have their part in the lake which burneth with fire and brimstone: which is the second death.

Why would God mention the eight sins in this verse out of all the other sins? I believe it is because the eight sins listed are so seductive and addictive that sinners will choose them over redemption.

Have you ever tried to witness to a drunk person? I have many times. It is almost impossible for them to grasp the peril of their condition and the beauty of salvation. Countless sinners are drunk with sin and pleasure in our modern age. As a result, death will be upon them without them ever considering the seeking Saviour or their sinful soul. They will open their eyes in Hell without Christ, being in eternal torment. How sad!

Luke 21:34

And take heed to yourselves, lest at any time your hearts be overcharged with surfeiting, and drunkenness, and cares of this life, and so that day come upon you unawares.

41

2. Strongholds of the Mind.

The battlefield for the souls of men is the mind. The law of sin operates in our flesh. The law of Satan attacks the mind.

Romans 7:23

But I see another law in my members, warring against the law of my mind, and bringing me into captivity to the law of sin which is in my members.

When people lose the battle of the mind, sin runs rampant in the flesh.

Satan builds strongholds, or castles of fortification, in the mind. From these strengthened positions, he wages war upon the mind and soul. The weapons of his warfare are imaginations (pictures and stories) and lies that contradict what we know to be true about God.

Unbelief is the crown of satanic endeavor. His goal is to take as many souls to Hell with him as possible. Unbelief causes people to go to Hell. People don't go to Heaven because they are good, and they don't go to Hell because they are bad. Ultimately, people go to Heaven because they accept Jesus Christ as their Saviour, and they go to Hell because they reject Him in unbelief.

John 3:18

He that believeth on him is not condemned: but he that believeth not is condemned already, because he hath not believed in the name of the only begotten Son of God.

If the Devil fails to keep one from being born again, He immediately begins working to paralyze the believer from meaningful service to God. Once again, the main goal is unbelief. God will not work mightily unless His people have faith.

Matthew 13:58

And he did not many mighty works there because of their unbelief.

Satan erects strongholds in the mind to protect and promote doubt and unbelief. Consider the following examples of satanic strongholds. Meditate upon how these sinful attitudes could keep a sinner from trusting Christ.

1. Greed.

2. Bitterness.

3. Addiction.

4. Pride.

5. Lust.

6. Fear.

7. Hatred.

8. Idolatry.

9. Dishonesty.

10. Covetousness

The Enemy can manipulate any sin to keep someone from trusting Christ. When working with a sinner, it is vital to identify the stronghold hindering them from trusting Christ. Use Scripture to refute the lie. The truth always makes people free when it is embraced.

The doctrine of RANSOM is an important concept regarding our salvation. This word is used sixteen times in the King James Bible. The doctrine of ransom states that sinners were kidnapped by Satan and bound by sin. Jesus Christ sacrificed Himself for our deliverance. He became the ransom. His death, burial, and resurrection was the price that was paid purchased our eternal freedom.

Mark 10:45

For even the Son of man came not to be ministered unto, but to minister, and to give his life a ransom for many.

1 Timothy 2:6

Who gave himself a ransom for all, to be testified in due time.

Satan is the evil captor of billions of people. Christ has paid the price for their salvation. Only by overpowering Satan with the spiritual weapons of warfare can we rescue sinners from his diabolical clutches.

5

Our Weapons Of Spiritual Warfare

Since soul winning is spiritual warfare, we must familiarize ourselves with the spiritual weapons at our disposal to win the battle for souls.

2 Corinthians 10:3–5

For though we walk in the flesh, we do not war after the flesh: (For the weapons of our warfare are not carnal, but mighty through God to the pulling down of strong holds;) Casting down imaginations, and every high thing that exalteth itself against the knowledge of God, and bringing into captivity every thought to the obedience of Christ;

Thankfully, Christ gave us spiritual weapons to rescue people from the clutches of their spiritual abductor. Just as a soldier must learn how to handle his rifle, use a grenade, or request air support, likewise believers must learn how to use the spiritual weapons we have been given.

Study the following weapons of spiritual warfare and use them to fight for lost souls in prayer and soul winning.

1. Fullness of the Holy Spirit.

Acts 1:8

But ye shall receive power, after that the Holy Ghost is come upon you: and ye shall be witnesses unto me both in Jerusalem, and in all Judaea, and in Samaria, and unto the uttermost part of the earth.

The Holy Spirit is God's gift to the redeemed. He is the engine of all spiritual power in our lives. We can't accomplish anything supernatural without his power.

Everything that Jesus Christ did while He was on earth was accomplished through the power of the Holy Ghost. He was filled with the Spirit without measure.

John 3:34

For he whom God hath sent speaketh the words of God: for God giveth not the Spirit by measure unto him.

As our example, Christ taught us that we must be filled with the Holy Ghost to accomplish His supernatural works. The Holy Spirit is God in us. He is our Partner in spiritual warfare. We must seek His fullness and yield to His leadership.

2. Persevering Prayer.

Ephesians 6:18

Praying always with all prayer and supplication in the Spirit, and watching thereunto with all perseverance and supplication for all saints;

Prayer is the "air support" of spiritual warfare. Every seasoned soldier knows that whoever controls the skies will probably win the battle. An airstrike softens targets for a ground assault. Only a fool would storm the enemy with ground troops alone when air power is available. We must pray!

Prayer can go where you cannot. It works while you are asleep. Its power cannot be denied.

Satan has no defense against prayer. Satan is winning when we aren't praying. When we are praying, Satan is losing. No wonder he works so hard to disrupt our prayer lives!

We must engage in persevering prayer! We must plead with God fervently until the answer comes.

Abraham pleaded for Sodom in Genesis eighteen.

Moses pleaded for Israel in Exodus thirty-two.

Hezekiah pleaded for Juda in II Kings nineteen.

The Bible is full of examples of those who won significant victories in persevering prayer.

Consider the unmatched power of prayer in Isaiah chapter thirty-seven.

> *Isaiah 37:36*
>
> *Then the angel of the LORD went forth, and smote in the camp of the Assyrians a hundred and fourscore and five thousand: and when they arose early in the morning, behold, they were all dead corpses.*

In answer to the prayers of King Hezekiah and the prophet Isaiah, the Lord sent an angel who killed 185,000 Assyrians in one night. To put that into perspective, the atomic bomb the United States dropped on Japan during World War II killed around 92,000 people. One angel killed twice that amount in one night. This Scripture reveals that Hezekiah's prayer was twice as explosive as an atomic bomb! Nothing in this world is more potent than persevering prayer.

God loves to answer the prayers of His children. We must pray for the lost as if their souls depended upon it-because they do!

3. The Word of God.

Ephesians 6:17

And take the helmet of salvation, and the sword of the Spirit, which is the word of God:

The Word of God is the sword of the Holy Spirit. The Spirit uses the Word to convict and convert sinners.Prayer and the Word of God are the only two offensive weapons mentioned in Ephesians chapter six.

God's Word always does its job. It never returns void.

Isaiah 55:11

So shall my word be that goeth forth out of my mouth: It shall not return unto me void, But it shall accomplish that which I please, And it shall prosper in the thing whereto I sent it.

We should use the Word of God to pray for sinners to be saved. Then we must use it to preach the glorious Gospel of Christ to the lost.

4. The Name of Jesus.

The name of Christ is powerful! Why don't we use it more often?

Our Saviour taught us to pray in His name.

John 14:13–14

And whatsoever ye shall ask in my name, that will I do, that the Father may be glorified in the Son. If ye shall ask any thing in my name, I will do it.

The disciples performed miracles in the name of Jesus.

Acts 4:10

Be it known unto you all, and to all the people of Israel, that by the name of Jesus Christ of Nazareth, whom ye crucified, whom God raised from the dead, even by him doth this man stand here before you whole.

The enemies of Christ sought to restrict use of His name because of its power.

Acts 4:18

And they called them, and commanded them not to speak at all nor teach in the name of Jesus.

The disciples of Christ overcame demons through the name of Christ.

Luke 10:17

And the seventy returned again with joy, saying, Lord, even the devils are subject unto us through thy name.

We can use the name of Christ to bind the evil strong man.

Invoking the name of Christ is powerful for three reasons:

a. Christ is Lord through CREATION.

Colossians 1:16

For by him were all things created, that are in heaven,

and that are in earth, visible and invisible, whether they be thrones, or dominions, or principalities, or powers: all things were created by him, and for him:

b. Christ is Lord through CRUCIFIXION.

Hebrews 2:14–15

Forasmuch then as the children are partakers of flesh and blood, he also himself likewise took part of the same; that through death he might destroy him that had the power of death, that is, the devil; And deliver them who through fear of death were all their lifetime subject to bondage.

c. Christ is Lord through CORONATION.

1 Peter 3:22

Who is gone into heaven, and is on the right hand of God; angels and authorities and powers being made subject unto him.

There is no name like the name of Jesus! We must use it liberally in spiritual warfare.

5. The Blood of Christ.

Revelation 12:11

And they overcame him by the blood of the Lamb, and by the word of their testimony; and they loved not their lives unto the death.

The blood of Christ is the most powerful substance in the universe. It did what nothing else could do. It washed away our sins!

Job 25:4

How then can man be justified with God? Or how can he be clean that is born of a woman?

1 John 1:7

But if we walk in the light, as he is in the light, we have fellowship one with another, and the blood of Jesus Christ his Son cleanseth us from all sin.

Revelation 1:5

And from Jesus Christ, who is the faithful witness, and the first begotten of the dead, and the prince of the kings of the earth. Unto him that loved us, and washed us from our sins in his own blood,

We are cleansed by the blood of the Crucified One!

Hebrews 2:14

Forasmuch then as the children are partakers of flesh and blood, he also himself likewise took part of the same; that through death he might destroy him that had the power of death, that is, the devil;

Satan was thoroughly defeated on the Cross. He was embarrassed at the resurrection of Jesus. Pleading the blood of Christ reminds Satan that he is a defeated foe!

6. Supreme Love For Christ.

Revelation 12:11

And they overcame him by the blood of the Lamb, and by the word of their testimony; and they loved not their lives unto the death.

This powerful verse reveals three reasons why these

believers overcame the devil. The third reason is that they loved not their lives to the death. What does that mean? It means they loved Jesus Christ more than themselves.

Since these believers loved Christ supremely, they defeated Satan. The Devil's attacks, temptations, and distractions held no sway over them. If you love anything more than Christ, Satan will use it against you. Search your heart right now. Do you love Christ supremely? You can.

Invite Jesus Christ onto the throne of your life. Declare your fealty to Him alone. Choose to love Him above all else this life has to offer. Supreme love for Christ is a powerful weapon in spiritual warfare.

Mark 12:30

And thou shalt love the Lord thy God with all thy heart, and with all thy soul, and with all thy mind, and with all thy strength: this is the first commandment.

7. Authority in Christ.

Matthew 16:19

And I will give unto thee the keys of the kingdom of heaven: and whatsoever thou shalt bind on earth shall be bound in heaven: and whatsoever thou shalt loose on earth shall be loosed in heaven.

Mark 13:34

For the Son of man is as a man taking a far journey, who left his house, and gave authority to his servants, and to every man his work, and commanded the porter to watch.

Authority is a type of power. Consider the following illustration.

Picture an 80,000 pound cement truck driving down the highway at 65 mph. It has raw power. No man would have enough strength to physically stop it from moving. Now, picture a 200-pound state trooper stepping into the highway in front of the cement truck. As the officer motions for it to pull over, the truck begins to slow down, coming to a stop at the side of the road. Why? The truck had more power, but the state trooper had more authority.

God has given us authority! We not only have spiritual power through the Holy Spirit, but also we have spiritual authority as Christ's servants.

As a policeman directs traffic, we have the authority to pray for the redemption of lost souls, bind Satan, and demand their deliverance.

In the booklet, "Praying Effectively For The Lost," Lee Thomas made this observation.

> *"Legally, all souls belong to Christ because He paid for their sins on Calvary.*
>
> *1 John 2:2*
>
> *And he is the propitiation for our sins: and not for ours only, but also for the sins of the whole world.*
>
> *But Satan, illegally and forcefully, continues to hold them captive, resolutely refusing to let the go. And he will continue to hold them bound in spiritual darkness until we take our rightful place and exercise our spiritual rights by demanding their immediate release on the basis of Christ's shed blood and our delegated authority from Him."*

We must pray with authority for sinners to be saved.

8. Sincere Praise.

Psalm 22:3

But thou art holy, O thou that inhabitest the praises of Israel.

The Almighty gets excited when people praise His name. Do you like to be around negative people? Did you hang around with people saying negative things about you or disagreeing with everything you say? Of course, not. Neither does God!

In Second Chronicles chapter 20, Judah was being attacked by a combined army of several nations. The worried King called for all Judah to fast and pray. But it was only when they began to sing and to praise the Lord that He worked on their behalf.

2 Chronicles 20:22

And when they began to sing and to praise, the LORD set ambushments against the children of Ammon, Moab, and mount Seir, which were come against Judah; and they were smitten.

This story is a powerful reminder of the importance of praise in spiritual warfare. Stop acting defeated! Praise God for what He has done and what He's going to do. Sing and praise His name waiting for Him to work and then continue because He has worked mightily.

9. Earnest Fasting.

Christ's disciples could not cast out a particular devil from a young man who was in the clutches of Satan. The Lord explained that this kind of foe is especially difficult. Only through the multiplied power of prayer and fasting could they bind the strong man to save the child.

Mark 9:29

And he said unto them, This kind can come forth by nothing, but by prayer and fasting.

Fasting from food and pleasure is one of our most powerful spiritual weapons. It weans us from the intoxicating teat of worldly pleasure, reveals the weakness of our flesh, and drives us to rely upon God with an urgency that can come no other way.

Isaiah chapter 58 details the incredible power of fasting. Consider this verse.

Isaiah 58:6

Is not this the fast that I have chosen?

To loose the bands of wickedness,

To undo the heavy burdens,

And to let the oppressed go free,

And that ye break every yoke?

Fasting is a lost art among modern Christians. Yet, only through frequent fasting will we gain the spiritual power to overcome the increasing wickedness of this present evil world.

When was the last time you fasted for a lost soul? When was the last time you skipped some meals in search of spiritual power?

10. Genuine Tears.

Psalm 126 offers a proven plan for guaranteed soul winning success. It includes an item that will surprise most people.

Tears.

Psalm 126:5–6

They that sow in tears shall reap in joy. He that goeth forth and weepeth, bearing precious seed, Shall doubtless come again with rejoicing, bringing his sheaves with him.

How are tears spiritual? Because they flow from the heart. True compassion moves people to action. Moved with compassion by the crowds of sheep who had no shepherd, Christ did whatever was necessary to help them. Likewise, when God's people are moved to tears, they will pray for the lost and work to save sinners with an irresistible passion.

Too often, we look at the plight of sinners with sickening indifference. We act as if their condition is not our problem.

Too often, we live as though we can relax as long as our friends and family are safe. Not so! Christ made the salvation of sinners every believer's responsibility. We are accountable for the souls of men!

Mark 16:15

And he said unto them, Go ye into all the world, and preach the gospel to every creature.

How long has it been since you wept for someone who was one heartbeat away from eternal damnation? Probably too long. We must pray for God to give us tears for lost souls. We must follow the compassionate example of Christ to do whatever it takes to save sinners. Only then will we see the true power of God unleashed.

6

Praying Effectively For The Lost

Let's review what we have learned so far.

1. We Don't Pray Effectively For Sinners To Be Saved.
2. Salvation Of Sinners Requires A Miracle.
3. Salvation Of The Lost Is The Pressing Desire Of Christ.
4. Salvation Of The Wicked Is Spiritual Warfare.
5. God Has Given Us Ten Powerful Weapons To Defeat Satan.

Although we are focused on the powerful weapon of prayer in this book, I pray that you can see that God has not left us powerless. He has given us powerful weapons to win the battles of life and reach lost souls. Only through effective intercessory prayer can we rescue lost sinners from eternal damnation. In this final section, we will learn specific prayer requests that we can use to pray for sinners to be saved. These prayer requests are biblical, proven, and powerful. Our prayers can bind Satan, soften the heart, and bring conviction.

Ultimately, the final decision to accept or reject Christ is left to the individual. Nevertheless, our prayers can lessen the grip of sin, empower soul-winning efforts and multiply the harvest of souls.

How To Pray Generally for Lost People To Be Saved.

You should pray for the lost in your community and around the world to be born again. You may not know their names, but God does. You can pray for the Almighty to open their eyes, convict their hearts, and save their souls. God will set up divine appointments for soul winners to meet sinners under conviction to give them the Gospel.

Use these suggestions for prayer requests as you pray for lost souls you don't know personally.

1.

Pray for the Holy Ghost to work among sinners to soften hearts and open doors.

2.

Beg the Holy Spirit to convict them of sin, righteousness, and judgment.

3.

Pray for them to recognize the wickedness of their sin.

4.

Pray that they see the perfect righteousness of Christ Who is their Judge.

5.

Pray for them to sense their coming judgment before the Holy God of all Creation.

6.

Pray for God to rip the blinders off their eyes so they can see the light of the glorious Gospel of Christ.

7.

Ask God to bind Satan and his minions from working to keep the lost bound and blind.

8.

Rebuke deceiving spirits laboring to deceive the sinner in the name of Jesus.

9.

Pray that sinners would stop listening to people leading them away from God.

10.

Pray that they would acknowledge Jesus Christ as the virgin-born Son of God Who died on the Cross to pay for their sin and rose again.

11.

Quote Scripture when you pray.

12.

Pray for God to send soul winners to share the Gospel.

How To Pray Specifically For Lost People To Be Saved.

We can pray specifically for the people that we know personally. Friends, family members, co-workers, soul-winning prospects should be brought before the throne of God by name when pleading for their souls.

When praying for a specific individual to be born again, use the general requests above, then get more specific by adding the following requests.

1.

Pray for God to put a hedge of protection from satanic influence on them. Name the offenders if you know them.

2.

Pray for God to sanctify them (set them apart for salvation) with the Spirit.

3.

Pray for God to reveal their sinfulness and shine the light on their specific sins.

4.

Pray for God to reveal to you the strongholds keeping them from Christ so you can address them with God's Word.

5.

Pray for God to remove the pleasure from sin and make sin exceeding sinful.

6.

Pray for God to send believers into their lives to share and reaffirm the Gospel.

7.

Pray for their heart to be prepared to receive the Word.

8.

Beg God to remove their heart of stone and replace it with a heart of flesh. (Ezekiel 36:26)

9.

Plead for God to make the conviction so real and heavy that they cannot deny God's invitation!

10.

Demand the sinner be set free in Jesus' Name.

11.

Plead the blood of Christ to cleanse them.

12.

Ask God to do whatever is necessary in the life of the lost one to bring them to saving faith in Christ.
(1 Corinthians 5:5)

13.

Praise God for His Saving Power and for saving them ahead of time.

14.

Remind the Saviour how much eternal glory He will receive from their redemption.

15.

Beg for their soul with tears.

16.

Ask God to glorify Himself by publicly saving this sinner and empowering him/her to serve the Lord.

7

A New Commitment

Lost sinners will not be saved unless someone prays for them. You can be that someone!

How many more souls would have been saved if we had only labored in prayer for them? How many more needless deaths must occur before we grasp the holy urgency of praying for the lost to be saved?

Satan wins when we don't pray. Satan loses when we pray. It's just that simple.

Let's commit to pray more effectively for lost souls in three simple ways.

1. Pray daily that souls would be saved in general. Use the biblical prayer requests we offered to pray for sinners in your community and around the world.

2. Choose five people whom you will pray specifically for

their redemption. Enlist in the spiritual battle for their souls. Use every righteous weapon of warfare available to fight for their eternal destiny. Ultimately, the choice of salvation or damnation will be theirs. However, you should determine not to let them go into eternity without a fight.

3. Spread the truth about praying sinner to Jesus by sharing this book with other believers and by sharing the testimonies of lives impacted by your focused prayer.

Through this biblical method of prayer, God will allow you to see more friends, family, acquaintances, and strangers saved. S

hare your encouraging stories with us at **info@ soulwinningschool.com**. We may share your testimony to encourage other soul winners and give God glory.

May God bless you with power and joy as you reap a harvest of souls!

About The Author

Paul E. Chapman loves helping committed Christians reach their potential, increase their influence, and impact their world.

He has served as the pastor of Curtis Corner Baptist Church since May of 2004. He and his wife, Sarah, are blessed with three precious children. They live in a coastal community in the beautiful state of Rhode Island.

They have a passion to reach the lost Christ, to teach believers to live by faith, and to train God's people for the work of the ministry.

Sarah has had a unique blend of aggressive autoimmune diseases since 2008 that leave her bedbound 95% of the time in constant debilitating pain. Their family's testimony of faithfulness to God has been an encouragement to many.

Paul writes weekly on his website and uses his unique blend of talents for God through various ministries and enterprises.

Learn more at www.PaulEChapman.com.

thepaulechapman

More Resources Available
From Paul E Chapman

<u>Mini-books</u>

Ye Must Be Born Again

Abortion Atrocity

<u>Books</u>

Just Say No: 40 Days To Victory Over Sin

God & America

The Beauty Of Salvation: Marvel At God's Unspeakable Gift

Winning Souls Step-By-Step: Your Step-By-Step Guide To Win Souls, Bring Guests to Church, And Baptize Converts

Find books, Gospel Tracts, and minstry resources at
ADDTOYOURFAITH.COM.

Made in the USA
Middletown, DE
30 September 2023